What Bird Are You?

Written in Colorado's first Bird City.

poems by

Amy Bobeda

Finishing Line Press
Georgetown, Kentucky

What Bird Are You?

Written in Colorado's first Bird City.

Copyright © 2023 by Amy Bobeda
ISBN 979-8-88838-216-5 First Edition
All rights reserved under International and Pan-American Copyright Conventions. No part of this book may be reproduced in any manner whatsoever without written permission from the publisher, except in the case of brief quotations embodied in critical articles and reviews.

ACKNOWLEDGMENTS

For the birds who are also people who are also birds.

Publisher: Leah Huete de Maines
Editor: Christen Kincaid
Cover Art: Gail Ritchie & Amy Bobeda
Interior Art: Amy Bobeda
Author Photo: Jacob Fishel
Cover Design: Amy Bobeda

Order online: www.finishinglinepress.com
also available on amazon.com

Author inquiries and mail orders:
Finishing Line Press
P. O. Box 1626
Georgetown, Kentucky 40324
U. S. A.

Table of Contents

Genesis I-III 1
Colorado in November 5
Wednesday 6
In the Conversation of Death 8
Lost Words 9
The Day I Walked 10
The Eagle 11
Portrait of Daly City 12
When I was Born 13
Some People 14
The Conference 15
Acoma 17
The Birds 18
Manhattan Bird Alert 19
Wringer 20
The Cement Ship 21
In the Kitchen 22
Collaboration 23
Why Some Feathers 24
From the Giant 25
Still 26
My Mother 27
In Davis 28
Happy Trails 29
A Coffee Bowl 30
The Nightingale 31
On the Day Barry Died 32
Did you Know Parakeets 34
Goldfinches Bickering 35
The Lovers 36

The Starling	37
At the Shakespeare Museum	38
Prospect Park	39
Night Migration	40
For Days	42
Rose Moon	44
Sometimes They Kill a Loon	46
The Lovers II	47
My Father	48
To the Great Horned Owl	49
Sky City	50
To the Artists	54
The Way of Clay	55
In the Studio	56
What is an Archive	57
I Tell the Potters	58
Dreaming	59
They Say Everyone in New York	60
Where I Live Now	61
Along the East River	62
Valley of Birds	63
In the Valley of Birds	64
Sunset Beach	69
In the Driveway	70
Easter Sunday	71
Notes & Acknowledgements	73
About the Author	75

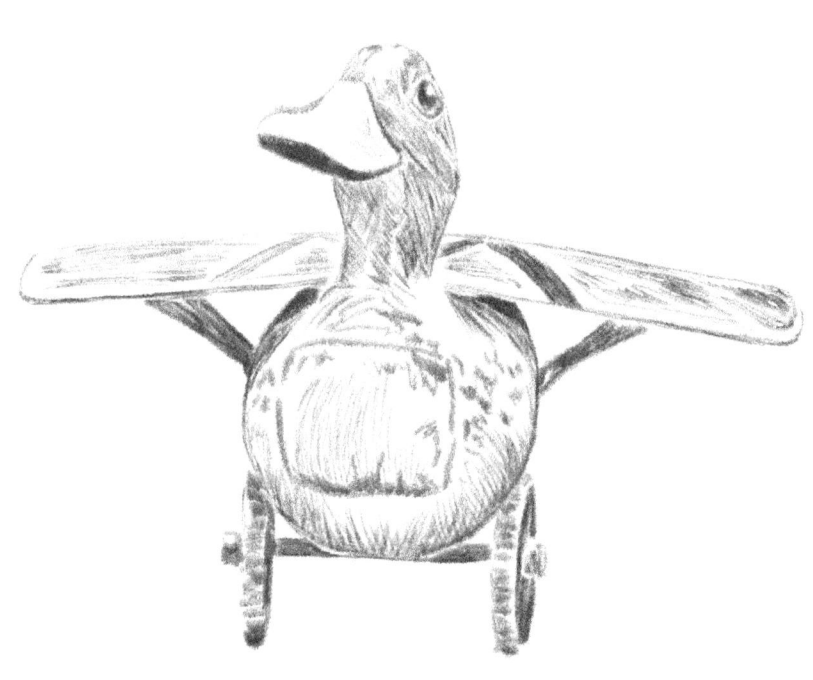

Genesis

I am reborn in books and oil. The anointment of Easter Sunday steeps tea in earthquake weather so still a little red plane coaxes clouds into new formations.

"The woman and man dreamed that god was dreaming about them," Eduardo Galeano writes in *Memory of Fire Genesis*. "In their dream about god's dream the woman and man were inside a great shining egg singing and dancing and kicking up a fuss because they were crazy to be born."

#

You text me, "did you know over 50% of the global population finds kissing disgusting?"
"How does that make you feel?"
"Like the time I learned the nuclear family was another lie."

My mother sends a photo: 4 Easter baskets filled with Reese's for my sister, her husband, my father and herself. I pour a vial of menstrual blood around a tree in the shape of an egg. I pull the Lovers reversed and wait for Lilith to devour me.

#

"We treat desire as a problem to be solved," Rebecca Solnit writes as the *Wall Street Journal* reports cargo ships off the shore of Los Angeles can't deliver imported teak furniture. "Desire makes everything blossom, possession makes everything wither and fade," are the only line of Proust I ever seem to remember.

Reading an old *New Yorker* essay in bed, my twenty-two-year-old self echoes between lines "All I want is a life in which I can read the *New Yorker* all day." That day is here! I later tell my mother. Her lips separate in a laugh and frown simultaneously. "For now," she replies. On the other end sculpting another beak, wing, shoulder, arm of a creature who will look so real when she is done, the world will forget how to animate itself.

#

In god's dream, happiness was stronger than doubt and mystery. When snake was born, god said, "here are 3 ships, two contain death." The snake watched the boats wash down river and picked the third. His immortality is the gift of rebirth: shedding skin.

#

I wake to news a series of earthquakes rattled Long Beach in my sleep. Dozens of cargo ships jiggle and roll across water waiting to deliver washing machines. The earth cracks open her egg. Warm and soft her yoke glows like the inside of a tree struck by lightning. The devil extends his hand. Job asks, "why does god give light to one who is in misery?"

The devil neglects to say, light transfigures magic from misery. The Piro of Peru call the airplane a "steamboat with wings," and say the paper is white man's mystery, the body of a woman alluring him to the page constantly each day.

#

In a dream the thread between you and me grows a snake from my womb. In the origin of rainbows seven balls of thread are thrown into the sky. All is warm. A parrot pricks a girl between her legs. For the first time women menstruate. A man sees the rainbow and falls down dead. For the first time people die.

"But they will be born again. They will never stop being born because death is a lie," god says.

Genesis II

god made man of clay
woman too, for some
reason forgot her vocal
chords, snake tried to
charm his way into her
voice but god said no, into
the blue extruder a lump
of earth pushes
the force of my
elbow, what comes out
looks like hair. god tells
woman to open her
mouth and I pour it down
like grandmother's
spaghetti until woman
sputters slip from her
teeth *I'll take it
from here.*

Genesis III

I was born of apple picking
people
sugar cane shucking
the sea between winter migration
and hibernating on the beach
when it rains

one day in my mining town
a dozen men opened the street

tore a black asphalt mouth
at my feet

a hundred thousand dragon flies
flew out

what is the difference between
a dragonfly and hummingbird feathering
from flower to flower
like light itself—the imago
from his cocoon, a well
cracked egg falling
into a tub of glaze

like my great grandfather
on the bayshore highway
toppling off the back
of his apple cart

Colorado in November

headlights fleck
black patches curving slick
the moon
extraordinary in its bloom
lights last marks of snow
by webbed feet

two by two geese
flee into
tracks melting under

I'll meet you here tomorrow
Jack says

the moon sheds crystals.

wednesday in the rose garden

moon, half-masked tips herself
into a cup, a single breast in deep
black water whence she cannot be pulled
back from the day. She unmasks a cardinal

bathing in the roseless garden, flapping through
the glass tumbler at Fishs Eddy, a Baltimore oriole
rests just long enough to squint a blush
of orange in the viewfinder.

I do not write about the moon because I can

without hardship
consistency & hope
oscillating
most days, it's all I can manage.

holy ghost

they say, when st joan
died a dove escaped
her gaping mouth

amongst flame &
flood

in search of land
to rest her dainty feet

an emblem of peace
where
there would be none
when
woman's wings
spring from coal
& kerosene
until she is so light
her ashen shadow
flutters in the
smallest breeze.

in the conversation of death

by her feet a steel machine
opens her windpipe
like the night blooming
cereus
her white petals glisten

the animal agrees or disagrees
to be
        taken

the dry earth drinks chicken
juice until her body, tossed into
the drum
of latex fingers rubs her
feathers clean off

Lost Words

in the hand
of a porcelain child my mother
sculpts a buttercup

she wonders what will become
of its petals without the thrush
wren, and magpie—

who will whistle through
the dandelion fields
but I love you still more than
anyone, darling

the day I walked the bkln bridge

I told myself *never again*
the eagle dipping his toes into the
reservoir at central park crowded by
cyclists, runners, and tourists circling so
loud not even the pickerel or carp
can be found.

the eagle with the sunlit eyes

I cannot help but think
your vagrant
tendencies are not
for social media fame
a bird's eye view of NYC
or ruse to escape
family—

instead, I have a hunch
you're fishing
Shakespeare's manuscripts
Spanish galleons
Portuguese casks
& Templar treasures
from myths
off the coast
of New Brunswick
before treasure hunters
find those too.

Portrait of Daly City

        My mother tosses the foldout couch
        over the balcony. My childhood bed
        flies into clumps of grass
        and sunflower hulls. The neighbors balk
        at her slight frame, white haired
        72 years of sculpted clay.

A man on methamphetamines drives down the alley at two
AM right into the trees my mother planted
to hide a slumlord rental.
The tow truck hangs over the gravel's
      edge. The high man jumps

    from
              roof   to   roof

until he breaks his foot   singing   the ambulance pools blood.

        A man hung on the fence, *these things happen*
        all the time, we just don't see
        them,
        my mother says.

A plumber comes to fix
the heater, across the street
the neighbor wields a two-by-four threatening to beat his car
if he doesn't move.

        My mother in her perch
        unrolls her swath of brushes. The legs
        of Sutro Tower sink
        into rocky soil, a finch flutters
        in the bird bath on the balcony
        where my mother tosses furniture.

When I was born

My mother taught me the language
of birds, her tongue a grosbeak

licking letters fingers
cast in slip hardening slivers

of porcelain hummingbird hovers
in the bathroom without a sip of sugar

water, an egret on the porch

sewn together with fishing line
a headless black swan

finally glued back together out by the pool
red marks of terracotta shining though

black glassy water in the sun. Once
there was a peacock stuffed in

the studio, a second chased
chickens round the yard always

escaping the neighbor's fence. The
moon accentuates her fingers

burnishing the eye so round
and bright the single tail feather

of the magpie dipped in lapis.

Some people go to therapy

Some people draw birds, my mother builds
wings, fashions ceramic pinions like an hourglass

grounded by weight, pinching perfect
glassy beaks and eyes suspending fragility

porcelain exceeds strength of bone
hollow, pressed together two concave bodies

become the breast of a single bird inhaling as her
lips blow air into the breast she slips the cavern closed

once she taught me how to make little heart shaped
pillows out of clay, staining my lips stoneware gray

I blew so hard the heart popped. She flattened it and
said *try again, but careful for air bubbles* which explode in the kiln

—what do they call it, wings against their
sides, ballistic with a small amount of lift—

an artery thrumming beyond skin veering
past the redwood into the kiln

a catacomb
bounding feathers.

The Conference of the Birds

The birds held parliament
eagle soared so high   from sight
clever wren hid under wing   to flit beyond eagle's beak

Ñiambiú declared herself   "daughter of misfortune"   her father
disavowed her lover 'til
    her   scream turned   people into willows she   a night bird
never hunted   often heard

    father says, "what the hell is moon water?"

another bow   boat   chalice scythes the sky
fingers   guzzling   full   moon below the firmament

jar of   driveway water   nests in   warm cracked tufts of crabgrass

Chang'e sought refuge   drank immortality   meant to share
with her husband and floated   into   space   Chang'e-5 collects LA LUNA
    bits
decoding origins

a woman has never touched the moon   let alone driven to her

acoma pottery workshop-california

John Bobeda on fri 30 aug 96

The University of California at Santa Cruz will be offering a one week workshop featuring internationally acclaimed Acoma Potters, Emma Lewis Mitchell and Dolores Lewis Garcia starting September 9th through 14th.

Emma and Dolores are daughters of the late Lucy M. Lewis of Acoma Pueblo, New Mexico. They have been featured in the late Rick Dillingham's books, "Seven Families in Pueblo Pottery" and the recent update, "Fourteen Families in Pueblo Pottery". They are also featured in Susan Peterson's book, Lucy M. Lewis, an American Indian Potter.

A video, "daughters of the Anasazi" offers an overview of their workshops, if anyone is interested in gaining insights into their lifestyle as Native American potters, living in a dual society.

I highly recommend this workshop for anyone interested in learning the "traditional" methods of producing Acoma black fine line designs on white forms.

The workshop will begin with forming techniques handed down from their ancestors. The workshop will include making traditional natural material, decorating slips, from local stone and plant materials, producing yucca brushes, burnishing, decorating steps with inspiration from Membres designs.

The workshop will conclude with a traditional above ground, oxidation dung firing. No prior ceramics experience is required. The cost is $325.00 and well worth in it. Unit credit of 2.5 quarter units is included.

My interest in this workshop is to promote the availability of information regarding these artists and their art. I have personally taken their workshops and found them profoundly educational and fun. I in no way profit from this workshop.

Anyone interested should call the University Extension Services Art and Design Department for information or telephone registration. I also can provide additional info by email.

John Bobeda
Ceramics Instructor
Cabrillo College

The Birds

The hummingbird is messenger
The crane immortal wing
The osprey stays away too long
The male crow cannot bring water people need
The female crow succeeds
The parrot is the child of gods' most useful woman
The condor was once a man who never stopped chasing a woman
The eagle was first shaman
The raven trickster and creator brought firelight
The owl most malevolent of all
The magpie is a fairy revel of sex
The dove becomes mother
The stork brings children
The pelican feeds young blood from her breast
The swan sings sweetly once in its life

Manhattan Bird Alert

Central Park snowy owl   track   map   tweet

five failed squirrel attempts   rat clutch   feet

adorable chickadee   peanut tounging   mitten seeds

      pond   pigeon mid-shred red-tail   lunch

camouflaged woodcock Bryant Park bound

Ramble barred owl boat house wavers   tufted titmouse retweets
all winter long

red necked loon
paddles

      great blue rising

 Pelham Bay
horned grebe

Harlem river   twice today

Shakespeare's garden thrush

shutter   click   tweet

Wringer

In my favorite dream outside the window
you turn into a golden eagle just as a kangaroo

hops by and I can't believe you miss it! I
run past a headless pigeon, his neck
overflows with seed my gullet fills

with pebbles, I try to swallow remembering
Palmer saved his pigeon Nipper, not once
but twice, and another boy asked his father for
a pigeon instead of wringing another neck so there is

hope for us
yet.

the cement ship, age 10

straddling Seacliff and Rio del Mar
I take my sister's picture
just before the fenced-off hull, her face
sepia like the pouch of pelicans
pirating the ship behind the fence
my father says *when I was a kid we could walk*
all the way to the end
I stick my nose in
chain link and enter the picture
in the county fair. For the next decade
when people ask *how old is your sister* I
say *twenty-seven* because the way her curls
meet the wind against the cement ship
twenty-seven forever.

in the kitchen

atop the fridge a basket of
unglazed eggs
someone says *may I have one*
they're not real
my mother says with a
glossy grin
on the counter a dish of
deviled eggs lined in
butterflies does not
spoil in afternoon
light

collaboration

my mother makes a honey dish
apple dipped white porcelain
my cousin's wedding gift
not old blue nor
borrowed with a golden stem
in the kiln the jar and lid
fuse—my mother holds the apple
under the tap and cries my father
takes it from her hand with a
single thwap—the burnt edge of
a wooden spoon the apple
blooms

Why Some Feathers Are Blue
Pima

like you
coyote longs to be blue

so he learns the song of
the blue bird
and practices until he too
is azul

so enamored with his own color
he falls into a coyote shaped
puddle
and turns the color of mud

inside each blue feather
particles separate water
evaporates
into pockets of air
which cancel out
every other shade

'til coyote realizes
blue is a structural color
and he is made of fur.

from the giant with 100 eyes

a white peacock preens her downturn
beak, drawing lines of sliver
clay, fingers dipped in
wax, I sculpt an eye, pressing
earthen metal into
a lattice of outlandish
lashes to wear around my neck
or dangle from an ear
guarding the gates of paradise

inside my cage
a fan of blue feathers settles
melts earth from metal in the kiln
reborn in precious sheen
of vision.

still

I want to sit in one place, writing
poems like the swallows nesting in the barn
across the street, their yellow bellies
pressing eaves as I sit
writing poems while someone else
pays for electricity. I never believed in
marriage because someone else would
pay the bills and I never leave
the nest, the barn collapsing
inside itself
devoured by the kestrel until
I am one wing.

my mother sculpts

a preschool
hollow stoneware
forms
a boy catching a frog dipped
in laguna's layered fern

a girl posing with a bird
each hair and feather scored
like dry riverbeds and all
I can think is this is how
she grieves mass-extinction

all the grandchildren
she'll never have.

in davis at the ceramics conference

on the Easter Bunny's lap
a polaroid of my heavy bangs

smiles and my mother swears
I loved that bunny so much

I wouldn't leave the store
to visit another gallery or

slip cast demo, one year I ask
if she will make a set of bangles out

of paper clay but she never does
because my father hid

the emersion blender he bought
her for Christmas to mix shredded

paper into porcelain, and he never
found it among the mess of wings

and noses in the attic, their students
always sculpting

rabbits, another year in a gallery
I find a perfect pink donut sprinkled

white and wish more than anything
it were real.

Happy Trails

January 1999, *Ceramics Monthly*
My father, who teaches ceramics, came up with this great idea for a slip-trailing tool. First, you need a bulb syringe that you can get at any drugstore, and a bicycle tire pump needle, called an inflating needle, available at sporting-goods stores and hardware stores.

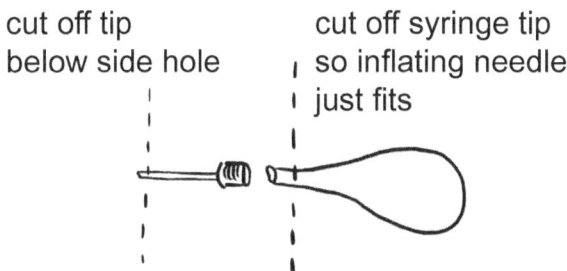

With a wire cutter, cut off the tip of the inflating needle just below the side hole, then reopen the flattened tip by squeezing the sides, using needle-nose pliers.
With scissors, cut the tip off the syringe, down to where the bigger end of the inflating needle will just fit into it. It should be a tight fit. Be careful not to cut off too much of the syringe tip, or the hole will be too big.
Fill up the syringe bulb by placing the opening in your slip container, squeezing and releasing, then insert the inflating needle and as my mom would say, "happy trails!"—Amy Bobeda, Corralitos, Calif. (age 10)

My first by-line was ghost written by a ceramicist five years after my father stuck a blue bulb syringe up my nose to extract gravel I believed belonged there.

The potter smiled, showing me the magazine clipping somewhere in Sedona where the rocks only smile terra cotta.

a coffee bowl, please

In the glaze room my mother says someone's made
glaze out of coffee mate creamer, dipping a cup into
a vat never knowing what color it will be when fired
so dull and chalky
like the rooster lying on his side in mud so still I
preserve his afterlife with a photo, my father
pours another afternoon coffee, always
half cold and black.

The Nightingale

On a soft red copy of Hans Christian Anderson from 1923 made out to a woman named *Constance* not my mother or her great grandmother of the same name lies a nest on its side carried in a bike pouch found outside the middle school, no birds in sight. I gave it three downy feathers from an eagle which is probably not legal, the shining black and green tail feather of a magpie, and one black feather with an orange stem I never identified.

On the day Barry died

her *new york times* obituary
said it's very rare for a celebrity
bird to die in a collision with
a park automobile, it is very
rare for a celebrity bird to have
her obit in the *new york times*

her glassy eyes canvasing the internet
hunting a token ride
from citibike
which might get me from bkln to
the park if I hurry and if traffic is
on my side
except for the part that on the day
barry died I'm in Colorado where a
young bald poops outside Walmart
before heading northeast
for barry's wake.

Did you Know Parakeets do not Mate for Life

Nikoline kept an aviary of pastel
parakeets and finches   the color
of the little blue treasure
chest she left me, one afternoon
in my thirties I drove to moss
landing to find her but couldn't
for the life of me remember where
she was buried and hoped
the internet would make it easier
to map the cemetery

too embarrassed to ask my father
who never talked about Nikoline
or her parakeets, I talked to the
entire

cemetery she did not wish
to be her resting place, like John's
headstone in Hawaii
a mass grave memorial outlined
in pulpy sugar

cane his parents farmed to gain
passage for two years I sift through
scythes and wide brim
shadows, turned
down mouths
like the honeycreeper's beak I
long to meet, before he too is
gone.

goldfinches bickering

200 starlings murmur
roof at dusk

red-tailed hawks nest
bathing white-throated sparrow

one of two turkey vultures
rescue escaped parrot in the park

grackle gives stink eye at duck
island

wings make notes a telling
machine

blue jays are often taken for
granted

spring time bathing at the loch
contrast grey on grey

fluttering over insects to perch

northern mockingbird holly tree
greater yellowlegs stalk
purposefully
tucking into a suet cake a couple
hairy woodpeckers

after hearing about glossy ibises
at turtle cove
new world warbler 5.15 pm

The Lovers

Folks ask how my summer was and I say
I had an affair with an eagle, sometimes
two when he would bring his tawny teen
whose crown hasn't turned to the tree
where we waste the afternoon next
to Walmart, longing to hug.

The Starling

The first starling arrived
in *Henry IV* act one
when Eugene loved
the bard so much
60 starlings filled the skies of
central park
never has a bird mentioned
once caused so much
trouble.

At the Shakespeare Museum

pillows of his face rest against
a dozen vases
crowd the dusty
place, just off the highway
in moss landing
where people stop for world-famous
fish stew and the view of
egret, heron, gull, and pelican
arguing with hamlet the
difference between hawk
and handsaw
as the otters clap
clams against their fuzzy
breasts
awaiting intermission

Prospect Park

tracing the lake with the subtle
color of a lady cardinal
beading glue along the edge of
another shattered bowl, trying
endlessly to meld my hardened
self into the softness of
a hand-thrown nest
with a bellow, the most
guttural cry
green night heron hollers
raaaaaaaaaaaaiiiiiiin, across the lake
lady duck burrows under
wing waiting for clouds to
menstruate until I am born

a fresh green lump
of muck and clay.

night migration

in the planetarium, erasing constellations
one by one the indigo bunting
loses himself among a
smattering of feldspar, talc
and cobalt carbonate. A sprinkle
of silica returns starlight

they say Polaris is the son
of moon and an unknown
father, like the bunting
always following the strongest
point of light between
exile and paradise a
great blue heron
in search of
deep water

for days, we cannot find the moon

1.

We sift the Manhattan skyline, incandescent
LED stars sieve and scatter
rats   across   the promenade—
Lady Liberty too, cannot find the moon
amidst her palm fire promising
what may never come.

2.

In a dream, you say you're looking at
the moon until it becomes the earth

when you try to take a picture, earth turns
into a billboard, the center of
Times Square, which might as well
be Las Vegas. Our bikes careen between
tourist traps   bells blazing
the shores of Manna-Hatta

sold for $24 worth of
beads and trinkets

the skyline clouds
pink, blue, red—whatever color
is on trend on the isle of Manna-Hatta
where we all become intoxicated on
neon letters, like the first time man saw
the moon scythe the night

and fell dead in surprise.

3.

five goslings brood
cement and feathers between
bridges, nothing
shelters wind from mother goose
her husband
too
cannot find the moon above
a streetlight glares into
the bit of river

rose moon

pink and bulbous, you neon
summer's dusky haze
drop a feather in the gutter
longer than my arm, I twirl
inspecting perfection
a few notches along the vent
ensure it's real, yet in the sky
I only see the blush of your
face, almost full of wonder

what a funny bird you are, god says
as I stick it to my tail with a wiggle
and a two-step the evening pavement
warms my toes until I take the feather
to my fingertips, arm outstretched—

—I lift—

sometimes they kill a loon who dances like a mad woman

California Modoc

loon woman wore the hearts of her family
under her neck scruff
like little red raisins

til one day

near the edge of the lake
an arrow pierced her chest

                    right, left, an erratic
                    circular dance

she died and was
reborn a wanderer

seeking amends
brewing medicine

loon woman set the earth
on fire, lightning poured
through
the smoke hole
gasping

she sings

charcoal melodies
of unrequited love

The Lovers II

First time I saw a cardinal, fall
you held my hand
in the Ramble, I thought it wasn't
real so pristinely crested
Icarus must not have
known
what goes up
must—

My father

His homemade 3-D printer
whirrs in the attic lining strings
of plastic on top of themselves
on top of a mirror, from the ceiling
an orange and white glider dust covered
from childhood, my old bed a pillow top hanger
so many tiny planes crowding
blankets, in the afternoon he flies them
with another potter in the east remote
lot near Kresge College where he taught
so many years ago I don't believe it when
he tells me just like the ceramic hang gliders
bound in shipping crates I've never seen
Dedalus without a son build wings

to the great horned owl in the ditch

I saw you coming round the bend
your wing askew, in a wave or
warning, in a dream you return me
to my grandmother's bed—the crossword
in her hand. On Sundays, they say it's
easier to fill, so many of us
scribbling our collective names, like
snake coiling upon himself into a little pot
or jug to dry leather hard, as you do
in the sallow-grass stun-dead

you ask if I could take your talons
—for a friend

I ask if
you are bringing death.

Sky City New Mexico

1.

orange ground
from stone painted with a yucca brush
tastes just
like it sounds, spitting
yuck -uh, chew the stem a while
softer

2.

The mesa forest consists of a single tree
her shadow fingers a dish of frybread a
nine-year-old girl carries paper towels
a bear of honey

3.

Dolores pulls a parrot from
her mother's old
train case

4.

Unwraps it as I remember
Osprey mate for life migrate
alone return
to the same tree on the
same day as last spring

5.

A man brings the chief
two eggs
one of parrot, one crow

Dolores pushes the basket
toward my hand
Indian Easter comes a week early
she says, a blue-brown warm
egg nests my palm

6.

A bookseller in Santa Fe hands me
Penguin Classic's Acoma mythology
whispers *this is a book of secrets and
controversy they never should have published*
I tuck it in my bag later a box
carry it across country only managing
to touch the parrot glossing the
cover

7.

The chief wanted a reservation full
of parrots so he threw the prettier egg
against a rock, a dozen of crows
flew out

8.

If you want a parrot you must
paint him yourself, Dolores
paints a tray of turtles she's
selling to the Met; I imagine
my friends on Fifth Avenue
slipping a bright white turtle
wrapped in tissue into
little leather purses

9.

This is how they did it she says
squishing overripe seeds of a

strawberry between her teeth
before
I crack open the egg, ancient
pottery secrets spill from
the train case into my ear

10.

Her mother watches
in an unmarked mesa grave
a photo of my sister buried
with her for a reason I may never
understand, in Manhattan I point
to a pot entombed in
glass and say, *That's one
of Lucy's,* the first woman
was the first potter

11.

My mother canvases the pasture
collecting cow pies in a garbage bag
Dolores and her sister are visiting
at the University we pile dung on top of
pots smoking themselves coal

12.

Dolores says in Sky City grandchildren
won't learn the language or how to
chew a brush, the day I write
this the Met turns 151 a fraction of the
time it takes a parrot to reach the moon

13.

The parrot's egg was black like a pit
fired seed pot so glossy in the sun

it reflects a rainbow and through
the tiny hole sprouts rain

14.

how do you know you are a bird? the parrot
asks
because you can paint

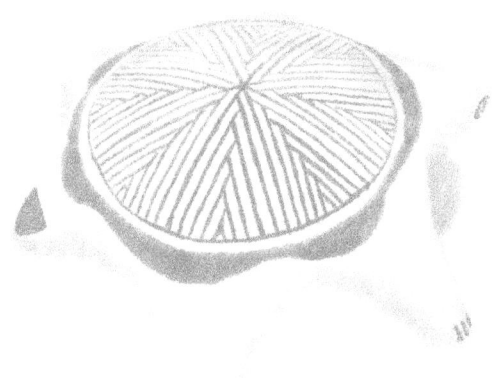

to the artists who chartered birds

birds mysteriously died from a blight
so uncharacteristic no ornithologist could

identify their tongues curling dry piles
on the highway rerouting boundaries

of life and death sucking
songs through airwaves aerosol cans hissed

spattered, blurt birds out their spouts
on roll-down doors throughout

Manhattan. Each urban memorial rolled up
and down around itself metal scratching

air so quiet bodegas began to whistle
first a bit of starling stammer and chickadee

reprieve each night drawing down corrugated
metal to sharp feathers of teenage night

heron's eyes, the envy of every street light
whistling a little song of northern thrush

or cardinal, the thump of the woodpecker
rattling another door, dappling the breast of

northern flicker black white dab of red
shouldering a blackbird dash so elegant

like the last standing chestnut tourists began
to whistle melodies unforgotten beaking

over the sea doctors sang regent honeyeaters
back to memory until the air so full of chatter

the pelican's pouch overflowed with ducklings
grebes, storks and loons.

The Way of Clay

potters always say if it doesn't explode
in the kiln
fuse together
shrink
if the slip and scoring do not hold

smash it

when a hummingbird drinks
honey, her tongue swells beyond
her beak until she can no longer
feed

the male hummingbird wastes
his energy each second waiting
for a woman to take him
into her nest-making

potters say
even the most precious pieces
break

eventually.

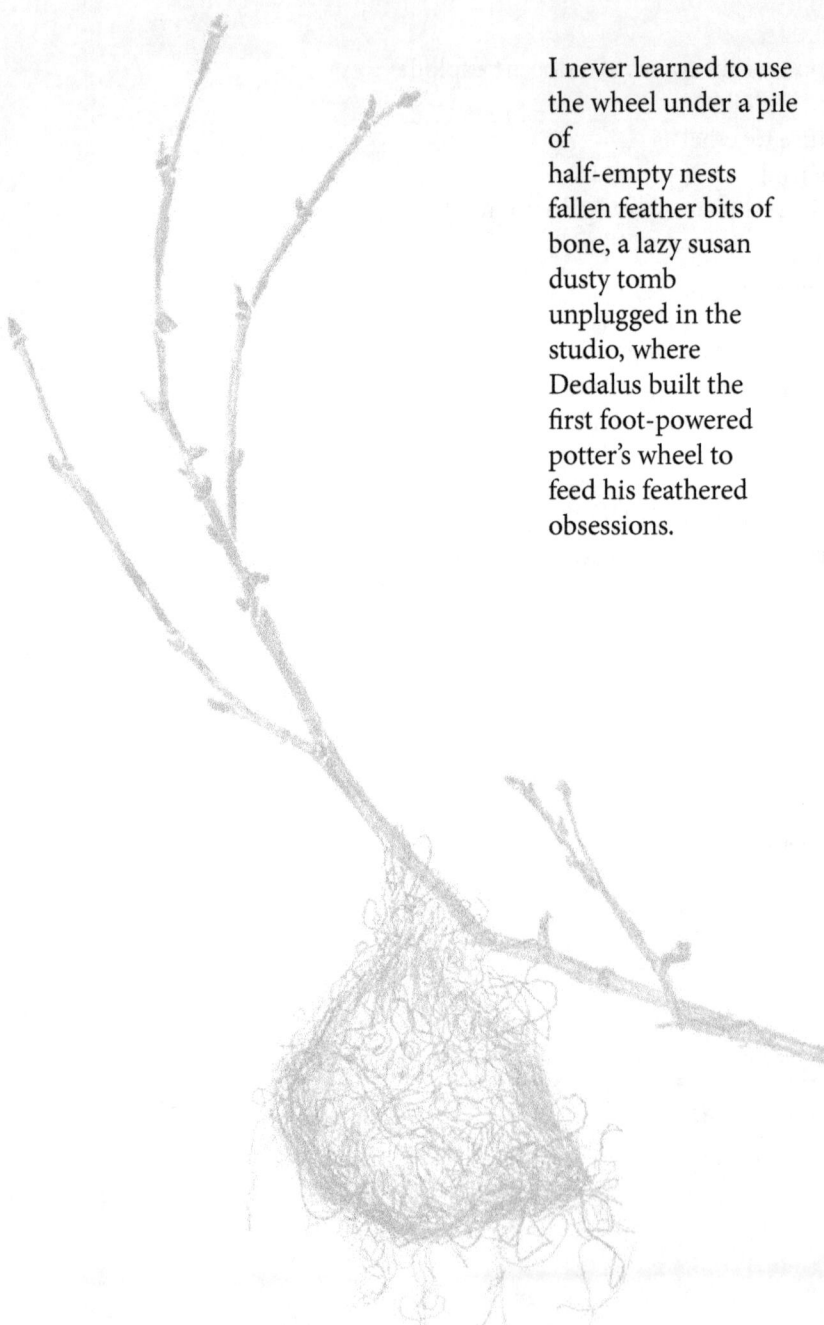

in the studio

I never learned to use
the wheel under a pile
of
half-empty nests
fallen feather bits of
bone, a lazy susan
dusty tomb
unplugged in the
studio, where
Dedalus built the
first foot-powered
potter's wheel to
feed his feathered
obsessions.

What is an Archive?

Sun-stained   strands
                a birthday ribbon
                            unpaid debts
                                      dismantling the nest
                                                until spring comes again.

I tell the potters
I'm teaching Manifestos

to young poets and the potters say
*I never met a manifesto that didn't
scare me* and my students say
what's a manifesto anyway?

while potters press
manifestos with finger
pads and nail beds—so strong
and ancient
glyphs
pouring water through
our lips.

Dreaming In the North Woods

eager to meet an expectant mate—
like the boy in Central Park eyeing
a black-haired night heron's crest
wobbling his hair feathers, crying

You have not called in weeks, my mother
exclaims, my father so distraught he
jumps into a little red airplane
buzzing my ear like a dragonfly

which cannot hear his plight
from a rock too far
fraught to comprehend our distance—

a heart-hanger hovering
in wait

they say everyone in New York has a book deal

from the window
all I see is steel: the lattice

brick: scaffolding

wheels clanking
steel plates, drumming

helicopters singing
into every atom.

I migrate home
where I may miss cardinals
of central park
hawks hunting kids at NYU
green night herons
keeping bkln safe from
incoming rain

which falls less and less
here among magpie
wings, kestrels hunting prairie dogs
great horned owls floating
in
midnight swaths of air

where I live now

struck
by lightning
a tree
liquifies
&
explodes

I question chance

on the corner
of Etna
and Icarus

a red tail
claws
the lamppost like
a rattlesnake
writhing

through my window
never knowing
warmth.

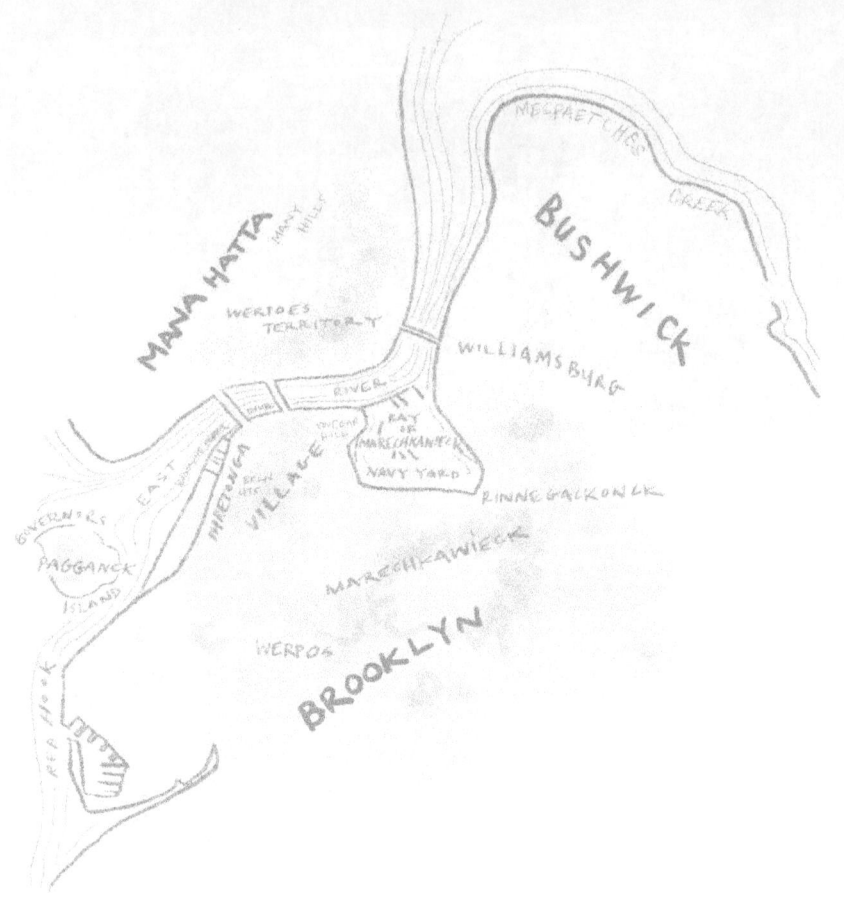

Along the East River

heaps of goose shit and   flecks   of gold confetti   dusted into pans,   under bushes
domesticated   by men stoned   with brush and bucket   harvesting tourist trash
   longing to be   not of service   but of river
   her dirty tongue   turning   the ferry bilge
                     as the firemen's tug
                  churns
   licking   oil slick cormorant   necks until they too   are river.

Valley of Birds

gathering tule stocks
their insides a spongy
marrow of
a black bird's leg

I wonder what it is to build a nest
strapping tule into a canoe

so airy it could float across
the slough, under Main
Street south past the Target
built on Costanoan burial
remains, down the Pajaro until
I reach the Bay

three egrets raise their canopy
of wings, Rancho Juristac's
golden grass waves, for so long
they want to dig a quarry, mine
gravel and sand, an empty grey
pit
never
a place to nest.

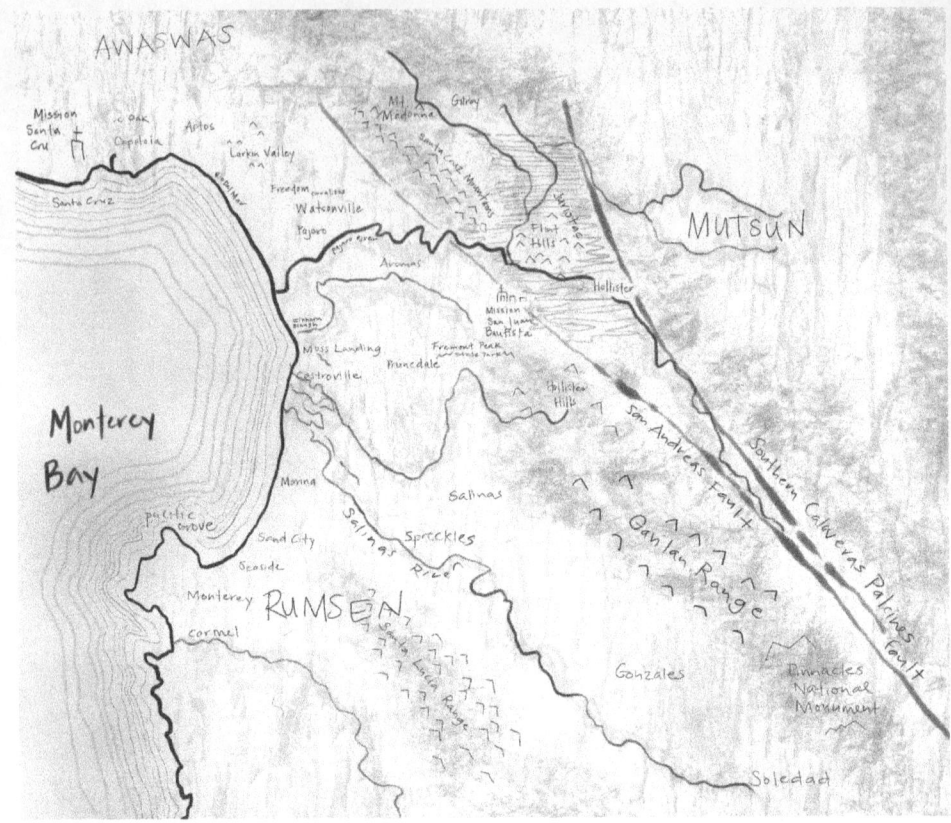

In the Valley of Birds

I was born in the Valley of Birds, just like my father. My mother, a Hummingbird flits around the yard, studio, classroom most days yearning for birds of San Francisco. Parrots of Telegraph Hill, great horned owls of Golden Gate Park, little round Presidio plovers, and feeders outside her Daly City window. Instead, she fills another jug of warm sugar water, cleans the feeders with a spiney bristle and waits for orioles on the patio.

Hummingbird's throat, they say, is red from carrying fire in her beak, bestowing humans with the gift of flame. There is a photo of my mother backpacking in Yosemite when she used to run with the rock climbers, before Royal Robbins started his clothing line. A red and black flannel curves over her shoulders. In summer she teaches watercolor to tourists in Yosemite Village and introduces her best friend, Judi to her future husband. Her front leg is poised to move. How rare it is, to find Hummingbird standing still.

It is Hummingbird who tells Coyote how to impregnate the first woman after the flood recedes and the Ohlone return to the Valley of Birds. In fifth grade, we watch a video on tsunamis in Hawaii and plan evacuations to the highest local point: Mount Madonna. My parents and I take Emma and Dolores to the Mount Madonna Inn for dinner when they visit from Acoma to teach a workshop on traditional pit firing. Other times, riding down the mountain from Gilroy, we pull over the car into the narrow parking lot on top of Mount Madonna to watch the sun sink over the Valley of Birds, where my father and I were born Coyotes.

We watch the video a second time in sixth grade as my mother helps me sculpt a replica of King Tut's death mask because the only thing I know for sure is that I lived in the Valley of Kings at the end of the 18th Dynasty. My mother does not question my fascination with my past life in Ancient Egypt, brushing a pearly suspension of gold upon Tut's nose. My father is in the garage, wishing he were a bird.

After the great flood, Coyote repopulates the Valley of Birds. When the water recedes, a young girl stands in the sand and Eagle says, "You must father her children." Coyote had no idea how. Hummingbird says, "In the belly, of course!" The girl eats a louse off Coyote's fur and turns into a shrimp. Things don't work out with Coyote's first wife; when I am born, I have a sister. My sister is born just north of the Valley of Birds where the Ohlone flee to Fremont Peak during the great flood. My sister is born human, and Eagle says, "Welcome."

Like Joan Didion, my father marries his first wife at Mission San Juan Bautista to appease his Spanish Catholic family. Like my sister, they are human. He marries my mother some years later off a cement-cracked patio where feeders hang from several trees and my mother fashions bird baths in every shaft of sunlight. She and the birds of San Francisco get tipsy the night before off brandy-soaked frosting. Stacking tiers of cake, they realize ceramicists are not bakers. My parents say their vows on patchy grass over the septic tank of the little red 1920's Sears Catalogue house with a paddock in back, in the unincorporated township Corralitos, meaning *little corral* in Spanish. Across the street cows, horses, and occasionally a llama greet us when we collect the mail. A single palm tree in the driveway marks which house is ours.

Before the flood, my parents live in a house built around a tree above the Soquel Creek which rises into a river when the great rains drive Coyote and

Hummingbird to a little coral next to the Harvest Moon Market where Bazooka bubble gum will always cost a quarter. "This," they think, "is the place to raise a daughter."

Coyote is a trickster. His sleight of hand manifests magic from nothing. For a time, the paddock becomes a foundry and we cast little toys and machine parts out of piles of Pepsi cans while my mother weeds black widow spiders from the giant ceramic robot under the sycamore tree.

When he retires from thirty years teaching ceramics, my father buys a model T speedster with bucket seats and we cruise through Watsonville, Gilroy, all the way to Fremont Peak; bugs fill our teeth. There are so many old cars in the yard I lose count except two El Caminos under the walnut that bears the least amount fruit and the '32 Ford in the garage the color of rust we haul from Arizona when Randy is finally presumed dead. Randy was a back country ranger who gave me books on animal wildlife every year for Christmas. It took five years to find a single bone most likely gnawed by a bear. At his memorial in Sequoia, I buy a teddy bear at the gift shop and rub my thumb into his plastic nose. "The disturbance of bones means the spirits are not at rest," an Amah Mutsun man says when Ohlone bones are unearthed across Santa Cruz county. I search every book for a story of a bird born from a man's bone; all I find is Eve.

The first time we go to Acoma to visit Emma and Dolores I am nine. On the Mesa the tour guide says, "those who refused to carry wood up the mesa first lost a hand, and then a foot." I stare at the church ceiling thatched in hand-milled logs. On the floor, a mountain of hands and feet glow red against the votive stand. That night I get so sick, I worry I will die in Sky City New Mexico whose only bird is a clay parrot.

For many years after retirement the only clay my father will touch is long coils fashioned into digeridoos that collect in the family room until he takes up flint knapping. He pounds stone with stone like Coyote pounds a six-legged man so flat he jumps on the back of a deer and becomes a tick.

What's always striking is the breadth of his abilities. In one story from the Northern Ute, Coyote fakes his own death and returns in a mountain lion skin to marry his daughter. His son gets suspicious when the mountain lion's teeth look just like his father's so their mother turns the family into stars and curses Coyote to solitude. In Navajo stories, Coyote creates the Milky Way out of impatience and is responsible for lunar phases. Sometimes, Coyote manifests havoc out of boredom.

Eventually, my father builds airplanes. Some the size of my mother's wingspan, some smaller. One day, while digging a trench in the back yard he says, "I always wish I'd been a pilot." In graduate school he makes ceramic hang gliders, now packed away in a shed. Coyote, always wants to be someone else, which is why he causes so much trouble.

In my thirties, I return to Sky City and ride the tour bus to the top of the mesa. For twenty years, the origin of Acoma's church is the only story I remember. A young woman gives the same speech—the hands, feet, and lives lost to the pueblo's largest building; a wooden crucifix so tall it reaches heaven. Above the door, I see a beautiful hand-painted rainbow. Above each window an animal or flower. "The church décor represents both Catholicism and our earth traditions," the tour guide says pointing at the yellow sun above the rainbow. In some stories, Coyote, Eagle, and Hummingbird go away. Perhaps they grow old and die, or seek a new life beyond the Valley of Birds. Perhaps the represent history misremembered as disappeared.. Sometimes a new story rises from old bones.

One night in second grade, Hummingbird and Coyote take me to the jazz club for some family-friendly folk only potters in plaid that smells like raku listen to. We run into Randy who's supposed to be in Yosemite. He's with a blonde woman I've never met. In *The Last Season*, Eric Blehm flourishes this scene, writing my mother "believes in fate," before she calls Judi to tell her of the affair. I flip through a copy of the book in the Ansel Adams Gallery in Yosemite Village. I rub my finger across my mother's name, yards from where she paints all the years before I'm born; I wonder if Hummingbird feels responsible for Coyote's first wife becoming a shrimp.

A friend tells me what she most admires about California shorebirds is their ability to coexist; their beaks divinely shaped to scavenge they don't need to compete with other species. A shore bird never wants to be another bird. In 1769 Portola and his men see a giant bird made of straw on the banks of the river and name it *Pajaro* as they cross into the Valley of Birds, *Popeloutchom* which stretches from Monterey to San Francisco. Less than a decade later, in the week of June that falls between my birthday and my father's, the adobe church at San Juan Bautista is built. Sometimes the devil himself appears in Coyote fur.

In Sedona, wind washes shards of pottery to the earth's surface. I collect them in my palm and run inside the house to show Coyote, Hummingbird, and Judi, before we haul the '32 Ford back to California. I never knew Randy was a writer despite Wallace Stegner suggesting he "try something else." His most famous work, a hand written note on the door of the ranger's station asked people to pack their trash. Writing is like the mountain and a ball of clay. Once it has touched you, there is no escape. Coyote had no idea how to repopulate the world, but knows he must try until he's succeeded or dies. Randy's Christmas gifts, little books about racoons became a secret message between writers in the world of potters and birds.

One day, outside Mission San Juan Bautista where the cemetery is fenced from view, I lean against the locked gate and imagine all the Mutsun on the other side marked with a white-washed crucifix. My father talks to a guy about flint collecting. A rooster and three hens strut past, pecking bugs in the lawn. I stare at my hands, each line carving a mountain, valley, and word. I decide I no longer want to be a Coyote.

When the flood covers the shore of Central California, Eagle carries Coyote and Hummingbird to the top of Fremont Peak, to begin the world anew. "The least I owe these mountains is a body," one of Randy's journal reads. The Park Service reports Randy likely fell through a snow drift and was swept into a waterfall. When Aristotle said birds transfigure into other species when the seasons change, I knew the opposite to be true. The next day I was born an eagle.

Sunset Beach

I'm flying on the beach, my father tells me
on days the wind beats his tiny planes
into shallow banks of seaweed
he sits to watch the waves, a double-crested
cormorant spreads her pterodactyl wings

hovering

the raven sea;

I've never seen a bird that hasn't made
me want to live.

In the driveway

My father says *don't mix*
up your verbs and adverbs
in the review mirror
his arm around my mother

out the window
I cry

poet's don't really worry about those
sorts of things
waving
his arm a biplane wing wraps
round
her hair an egret's crest
grows into the wind as I
descend
the driveway

Easter Sunday

the parrot asks god how
badly he wants to be
born and god fills
the moon until
the sun crosses
the equator

we bury eggs in
the yard, equalizing
night and day
the parrot whispers
to god inside his egg
what bird are you?

soil turns the egg
lapis, cardinal, chickadee
worms dapple the surface
like the red tail's cheek

god longs to
be a glossy ibis wading
western marshes
but only replies

as long as I can fly

the parrot scrapes a
speck of clay from her claw
and blows until god's egg
gets so small and warm he is
born a fly
on the moon

some Piro say *the moon is a man
with no home, wandering*

and in no time, god dies
reborn
an ibis

Notes & Acknowledgements

Genesis credits Eduardo Galeano's *Memory of Fire Genesis*, and Rebecca Solnit's *A Field Guide to Getting Lost*.

Lost Words references Robert MacFarlane's *The Lost Words*.

Some People Go to Therapy was originally published in TYPO Magazine.

Colorado in November was first published in Visitant Magazine under the name *Headlights Fleck*.

The Conference of the Birds uses excerpts from the Penguin Classic translation of the Farid Ud-Din Attar poem.

Acoma Pottery Workshop can be found on Google, originally written by John Bobeda on a ceramics forum.

Sunset Beach & *In Davis* were first published in *Hobart*.

In the Planetarium was first published in *Ecotheo Review*.

Manhattan Bird Alert was originally published in Entropy's *The Birds*.

Wringer references the young adult book by the same name.

Happy Trails, Ceramics Monthly is taken from the January 1992 issue of *Ceramics Monthly*

A Coffee Bowl, Please's title references *Gilmore Girls*.

Sometimes they Kill a Loon who Dances Like a Mad Woman references *The Inland Whale* and *Indian Tales* versions.

The Starling: Starlings were mentioned once in Shakespeare and were among the invasive species introduced to Central Park in the late 1800's by Shakespeare fans.

The eagle with the sunlit eyes is the meaning of "sea eagle" in Gaelic. The poem references the sea eagle that traveled the eastern seaboard and the men searching for mythic treasure on New Brunswick's Oak Island.

The Shakespeare Museum references the Shakespeare Society of America Museum, open daily in Moss Landing, CA. The poem reference's Hamlet's line to Rosencrantz and Guildenstern: I am but mad north-north-west: when the wind is southerly I know a hawk from a handsaw" (2.2).

On the Day Barry Died is for Barry the Central Park barred owl who was killed by a Central Park conservancy vehicle in the early morning of August 6th 2021. Her autopsy showed high levels of rat poison which may have affected her early morning flight. The poem was first published in *Columbia Review*.

To the Artists Who Chartered Birds references the Audubon mural project of upper Manhattan.

In the Valley of Birds references Eric Blehm's, *The Last Season*. It was first published in *The Lumiere Review*.

Easter Sunday references Piro ethnography from Peter Gow's *An Amazonian Myth and Its History*.

All original illustrations. Thank you Gail Ritchie and John Bobeda for all the years in the Cabrillo Ceramics Studio and forgiving my messes; Megan for loving the cement ship in all forms of decay; Emma & Dolores, your descendants and ancestors for sharing the wisdom of yucca brushes and pit firing; Kitty McInerny for my first byline; Andrew Schelling & Emily Trenholm for helping dream these threads into a nest of ecopoetics; Kathy Kearns for diving into the world of Dedalus with me in Crete; Krys Ritchie for our trip to NM; Manhattan Bird Alert and Bird Twitter for keeping me perched in the world of birds during lockdown; RAG for mythic inspirations; and Jacob for your patience and care on all these birding adventures born into these blue-feathered poems.

To the ceramic's family, dears, and little dears—Bill, Claudia, Patti, Carol, Louise, Kitty, Judi, Kathryn—thank you. For Bob—our eternal neighborhood birder.

For updates on Project Juristac visit: https://www.protectjuristac.org

Amy Bobeda holds an MFA from the Jack Kerouac School of Disembodied Poetics where she serves as the Director of the Naropa Writing Center. She sometimes teaches writing pedagogy and process-based art. She's the founder of Wisdom Body Collective, a process-based artist collective and small press. She's the author and illustrator of *Red Memory* (FlowerSong Press) *mi sin manitos* (Ethel Press) and has a forthcoming book from Spuyten Duyvil. Her work has been featured in Columbia Review, Ecotheo Review, Denver Quarterly, and elsewhere. She's also a retired cosmetologist and costume designer who loves reclaiming and refashioning fiber arts. Raised on the Amah Mutsun land of the Pajaro Valley by two ceramicists she is often found running, walking, and following birds in landlocked places.

www.ingramcontent.com/pod-product-compliance
Lightning Source LLC
Chambersburg PA
CBHW031125160426
43192CB00008B/1117